Jazz Decades

30's

THIS PUBLICATION IS NOT AUTHORISED FOR SALE IN
THE UNITED STATES OF AMERICA AND/OR CANADA

WISE PUBLICATIONS
LONDON/NEW YORK/PARIS/SYDNEY/COPENHAGEN/MADRID

D1340465

30131 03159191 7

LONDON BOROUGH OF BARNET

BOROUGH OF BARNET
LIBRARIES DEPARTMENT

CRAMER   12-11-96

EXCLUSIVE DISTRIBUTORS:
MUSIC SALES LIMITED
8/9 FRITH STREET,
LONDON W1V 5TZ, ENGLAND.

MUSIC SALES PTY LIMITED
120 ROTHSCHILD AVENUE,
ROSEBERY, NSW 2018,
AUSTRALIA.

ORDER NO. AM92390
ISBN 0-7119-4466-0
THIS BOOK © COPYRIGHT 1996 BY WISE PUBLICATIONS

UNAUTHORISED REPRODUCTION OF ANY PART OF THIS PUBLICATION BY ANY
MEANS INCLUDING PHOTOCOPYING IS AN INFRINGEMENT OF COPYRIGHT.

COMPILED BY PETER EVANS & PETER LAVENDER
BOOK DESIGN BY PEARCE MARCHBANK, STUDIO TWENTY
QUARKED BY BEN MAY

PRINTED IN THE UNITED KINGDOM BY
CALIGRAVING LIMITED, THETFORD, NORFOLK.

Your Guarantee of Quality...
As publishers, we strive to produce every book to
the highest commercial standards.
This book has been carefully designed to minimise awkward
page turns and to make playing from it a real pleasure.
Particular care has been given to specifying acid-free,
neutral-sized paper made from pulps which have not been
elemental chlorine bleached. This pulp is from farmed
sustainable forests and was produced with special
regard for the environment.
Throughout, the printing and binding have been
planned to ensure a sturdy, attractive publication
which should give years of enjoyment.
If your copy fails to meet our high standards,
please inform us and we will gladly replace it.

Music Sales' complete catalogue describes thousands of titles
and is available in full colour sections by subject, direct from
Music Sales Limited. Please state your areas of interest and
send a cheque/postal order for £1.50 for postage to:
Music Sales Limited, Newmarket Road,
Bury St. Edmunds, Suffolk IP33 3YB.

Caravan

By Duke Ellington, Irving Mills & Juan Tizol

© COPYRIGHT 1937 AMERICAN ACADEMY OF MUSIC INCORPORATED, USA.
AUTHORISED FOR SALE IN THE UNITED KINGDOM OF GREAT BRITAIN AND NORTHERN IRELAND ONLY BY
PERMISSION OF THE SOLE AGENT, J.R. LAFLEUR AND SON LIMITED.
ALL RIGHTS RESERVED. INTERNATIONAL COPYRIGHT SECURED.

Moderately, quasi misterioso

Night _____ and stars a - bove that shine so

bright _____ The mys - t'ry of their fad - ing

light _____ That shines up - on our car - a - van. _____

Sleep _____

up - on my shoul - der as we creep _____

A - cross the sands so I may keep _____

This mem - 'ry of our car - a - van.

you _____ Be - side me here be - neath the

blue _____ My dream of love is com - ing true _____

_____ With - in our des - ert car - a - van. _____

Drop Me Off In Harlem

Words by Nick Kenny Music by Duke Ellington

© COPYRIGHT 1933 MILLS MUSIC INCORPORATED, USA.
CAMPBELL CONNELLY & COMPANY LIMITED, 8/9 FRITH STREET, LONDON W1.
ALL RIGHTS RESERVED. INTERNATIONAL COPYRIGHT SECURED.

Heav - en up in Har - lem.___ I don't want___ your Dix - ie,___

you can keep___ your Dix - ie,___ There's no one down in

Dix - ie who can take me 'way from my own Har - lem,___

Har - lem has___ those south - ern skies,___ they're in my ba - by's smile,___ I

9

Don't Worry 'Bout Me

Words by Ted Koehler. Music by Rube Bloom

© COPYRIGHT 1939 MILLS MUSIC INCORPORATED, USA.
CINEPHONIC MUSIC COMPANY LIMITED, 8/9 FRITH STREET, LONDON W1.
ALL RIGHTS RESERVED. INTERNATIONAL COPYRIGHT SECURED.

This is the one mo-ment that I thought I nev-er could live thro', But now some-how, that it's here, my dear, that fool-ish fear dis-ap-pears, And say-ing good-bye seems sweet. It's plain that Fate did-n't want us on a one way street.

East Of The Sun
(And West Of The Moon)

Words & Music by Brooks Bowman

© COPYRIGHT 1935 PRINCETOWN UNIVERSITY TRIANGLE CLUB.
PUBLICATION RIGHTS ASSIGNED 1935 SANTLY BROTHERS INCORPORATED, USA.
CAMPBELL CONNELLY & COMPANY LIMITED, 8/9 FRITH STREET, LONDON W1.
ALL RIGHTS RESERVED. INTERNATIONAL COPYRIGHT SECURED.

How Ya Baby

Words by J C Johnson. Music by Thomas Waller

© COPYRIGHT 1938 RENEWED 1965 DORSEY BROTHERS MUSIC INCORPORATED/CHAPPELL MUSIC COMPANY, USA.
DORSEY BROTHERS MUSIC LIMITED, 8/9 FRITH STREET, LONDON W1/
REDWOOD MUSIC LIMITED, IRON BRIDGE HOUSE, 3 BRIDGE APPROACH, LONDON NW1.
ALL RIGHTS RESERVED. INTERNATIONAL COPYRIGHT SECURED.

Georgia On My Mind

Words by Stuart Gorrell. Music by Hoagy Carmichael

© COPYRIGHT 1930 SOUTHERN MUSIC PUBLISHING COMPANY INCORPORATED, USA.
CAMPBELL CONNELLY & COMPANY LIMITED, 8/9 FRITH STREET, LONDON W1.
ALL RIGHTS RESERVED. INTERNATIONAL COPYRIGHT SECURED.

In A Sentimental Mood

Words & Music by Duke Ellington, Irving Mills & Manny Kurtz

© COPYRIGHT 1935 BY AMERICAN ACADEMY OF MUSIC INCORPORATED, NEW YORK, USA.
REPUBLISHED CONTAINING NEW COPYRIGHT MATTER 1935 BY AMERICAN ACADEMY OF MUSIC INCORPORATED.
SOLE AGENTS FOR THE BRITISH EMPIRE (EXCLUDING CANADA) AND EUROPE, J.R. LAFLEUR AND SON LIMITED.
AUTHORISED FOR SALE IN GREAT BRITAIN AND NORTHERN IRELAND ONLY BY
PERMISSION OF BOOSEY & HAWKES MUSIC PUBLISHERS LIMITED.
ALL RIGHTS RESERVED. INTERNATIONAL COPYRIGHT SECURED.

In a sen-ti-men-tal mood _____ I can see the stars come through my room _____

While your lov-ing at-ti-tude _____ is like a flame that lights the

you made this night a thing di - vine. _____ In a sen - ti - men - tal

mood _____ I'm with - in a world so hea - ven - ly, _____

_____ For I nev - er dreamt that you'd _____ be lov - ing sen - ti -

1. men - tal me. In a sen - ti - men - tal

2. me. _____

24

I'm Gettin' Sentimental Over You

Words by Ned Washington. Music by Geo. Bassman

© COPYRIGHT 1933 LAWRENCE MUSIC PUBLISHERS INCORPORATED, USA.
© COPYRIGHT ASSIGNED 1934 MILLS MUSIC INCORPORATED, USA.
DASH MUSIC COMPANY LIMITED, 8/9 FRITH STREET, LONDON W1.
ALL RIGHTS RESERVED. INTERNATIONAL COPYRIGHT SECURED.

In The Mood

Words by Andy Razaf. Music by Joe Garland

© COPYRIGHT 1939 SHAPIRO BERNSTEIN & COMPANY INCORPORATED, USA.
SUB-PUBLISHED BY PETER MAURICE MUSIC COMPANY LIMITED, LONDON WC2.
ALL RIGHTS RESERVED. INTERNATIONAL COPYRIGHT SECURED.

It Don't Mean A Thing
(If It Ain't Got That Swing)

Words by Irving Mills. Music by Duke Ellington

© COPYRIGHT 1932 BY MILLS MUSIC INCORPORATED, USA.
© COPYRIGHT RENEWED 1960 LAWRENCE WRIGHT MUSIC COMPANY LIMITED, 127 CHARING CROSS ROAD, LONDON WC2
FOR ALL TERRITORIES (EXCEPT USA, CANADA AND AUSTRALASIA).
ALL RIGHTS RESERVED. INTERNATIONAL COPYRIGHT SECURED.

Let's Dance

Words & Music by Fanny Baldridge, Gregory Stone & Joseph Bonime

© COPYRIGHT 1935 EDWARD B. MARKS MUSIC COMPANY, USA.
PEERMUSIC (UK) LIMITED, 8-14 VERULAM STREET, LONDON WC1.
ALL RIGHTS RESERVED. INTERNATIONAL COPYRIGHT SECURED.

Just For A Thrill

Words & Music by Lil Armstrong & Don Raye

© COPYRIGHT 1939 MCA MUSIC (A DIVISION OF MCA INCORPORATED, USA).
MCA MUSIC LIMITED, 77 FULHAM PALACE ROAD, LONDON W6 FOR THE WORLD (EXCLUDING
SOUTH AND CENTRAL AMERICA, JAPAN, AUSTRALASIA AND THE PHILIPPINES).
ALL RIGHTS RESERVED. INTERNATIONAL COPYRIGHT SECURED.

How could I poss-i-bly know? How could I have con-ceived it, that you'd try to hurt me so? I'd nev-er have be-lieved it. I was a fool, but you were

Moonglow

Words & Music by Will Hudson, Eddie de Lange & Irving Mills

© COPYRIGHT 1934 EXCLUSIVE PUBLICATIONS INCORPORATED, USA.
COPYRIGHT ASSIGNED 1934 TO MILLS MUSIC INCORPORATED, USA.
AUTHORISED FOR SALE IN THE UK AND EIRE ONLY BY
PERMISSION OF BOOSEY & HAWKES MUSIC PUBLISHERS LIMITED, LONDON.
ALL RIGHTS RESERVED. INTERNATIONAL COPYRIGHT SECURED.

Solitude

Words by Eddie de Lange & Irving Mills. Music by Duke Ellington

© COPYRIGHT 1934 MILSONS MUSIC PUBLISHING CORPORATION, USA.
SOLE AGENTS FOR BRITISH EMPIRE (EXCLUDING CANADA) AND EUROPE J.R. LAFLEUR & SON LIMITED.
AUTHORISED FOR SALE IN THE UK BY PERMISSION OF BOOSEY & HAWKES MUSIC PUBLISHERS LIMITED, LONDON.
ALL RIGHTS RESERVED. INTERNATIONAL COPYRIGHT SECURED.

Pick Yourself Up

Music by Jerome Kern. Words by Dorothy Fields

© COPYRIGHT 1936 T.B. HARMS & COMPANY INCORPORATED, USA.
WARNER CHAPPELL MUSIC LIMITED, 129 PARK STREET, LONDON W1/
POLYGRAM MUSIC PUBLISHING LIMITED, 47 BRITISH GROVE, LONDON W4.
ALL RIGHTS RESERVED. INTERNATIONAL COPYRIGHT SECURED.

Noth - ing's im-poss-i-ble I have found, for when my chin is

on the ground, I pick my-self up, dust my-self off, start all o-ver a-

-gain.　　　Don't　lose your con - fi - dence　if　you　slip,　be

grate - ful　for　a　pleas - ant　trip,　and　pick your - self　up,　　dust your - self　off,

start　all　o - ver a - gain.　　　　　　　Work　like a　soul　in -

Stars Fell On Alabama

Words by Mitchell Parish. Music by Frank Perkins

© COPYRIGHT 1934 MILLS MUSIC INCORPORATED, USA.
CAMPBELL CONNELLY & COMPANY LIMITED, 8/9 FRITH STREET, LONDON W1.
ALL RIGHTS RESERVED. INTERNATIONAL COPYRIGHT SECURED.

dra - ma, we kissed in a field of white, and stars fell on Al - a -

ba - ma last night. I can't for-get the

glam - our, your eyes held a ten - der light, and stars fell on Al - a -

ba - ma last night. I nev - er planned in my im - a - gi -

na - tion___ a sit - u - a - tion___ so hea-ven - ly,_____ A fai - ry land where no one else could

en - ter,___ and in the cen - tre___ just you and me, dear. My heart beat like a

ham - mer, my arms wound a-round you tight, and stars fell on Al - a -

ba - ma last night.   night.___

Sophisticated Lady

Words by Irving Mills & Mitchell Parish. Music by Duke Ellington

© COPYRIGHT 1935 BY GOTHAM MUSIC SERVICE INCORPORATED, USA.
FOR GREAT BRITAIN, IRELAND AND COLONIES (EXCLUDING CANADA & AUSTRALASIA) THE PROPERTY OF ATV MUSIC, LONDON WC2.
ALL RIGHTS RESERVED. INTERNATIONAL COPYRIGHT SECURED.

Stormy Weather

Words by Ted Koehler. Music by Harold Arlen

© COPYRIGHT 1933 BY MILLS MUSIC INCORPORATED, USA.
LAWRENCE WRIGHT MUSIC COMPANY LIMITED, LONDON WC2 FOR UK, BRITISH COMMONWEALTH
(EXCLUDING CANADA AND AUSTRALASIA) EIRE & CONTINENTAL EUROPE (EXCLUDING LATIN COUNTRIES AND SWITZERLAND).
ALL RIGHTS RESERVED. INTERNATIONAL COPYRIGHT SECURED.

Don't know why _____ there's no sun up in the sky, Storm-y weath-er, ___

since my man and I ain't to-geth-er, _____ Keeps rain-in' all ___ the time, _____

D♭ A♭ D♭ A♭ C♭7(♭5) B♭7 E♭7
All I do is pray the Lord above will let me walk in the sun once more. Can't go
A♭ A dim B♭m7 E♭9 A♭ B♭m7
on, ev-'ry-thing I had is gone, Storm-y weath-er, Since my man and I ain't to-
A♭ B♭m7 E♭9(♯5) A♭ B♭m7 E♭9(♯5)
geth-er, Keeps rain-in' all the time, Keeps rain-in' all the
1. 2.
A♭ B♭m7 E♭9 N.C. A♭ B♭m A♭ D♭ A♭
time. Don't know time.
pp

Summertime
(from Porgy And Bess)

By George Gershwin, Ira Gershwin, DuBose & Dorothy Heyward

© COPYRIGHT 1935 (RENEWED) CHAPPELL & COMPANY, USA.
THIS ARRANGEMENT © COPYRIGHT 1995 CHAPPELL & COMPANY, USA.
WARNER CHAPPELL MUSIC LIMITED, 129 PARK STREET, LONDON W1.
ALL RIGHTS RESERVED. INTERNATIONAL COPYRIGHT SECURED.

63

The Joint Is Jumpin'

Words by Andy Razaf & J.C. Johnson. Music by Thomas Waller

© COPYRIGHT 1938 RENEWED 1965 DORSEY BROTHERS MUSIC INCORPORATED/CHAPPELL MUSIC COMPANY, USA.
DORSEY BROTHERS MUSIC LIMITED, 8/9 FRITH STREET, LONDON W1/REDWOOD MUSIC LIMITED,
IRON BRIDGE HOUSE, 3 BRIDGE APPROACH, LONDON NW1.
ALL RIGHTS RESERVED. INTERNATIONAL COPYRIGHT SECURED.

Tempo di-sturb de neighbors

They have a new ex-pres-sion a-long old Har-lem way___ that tells you when a par-ty is ten times more___ than gay.___ To say that things are jump-in' leaves not a sin-gle doubt___ that

67

The Song Is You

Music by Jerome Kern. Words by Oscar Hammerstein II

© COPYRIGHT 1932 T.B. HARMS & COMPANY INCORPORATED, USA.
POLYGRAM MUSIC PUBLISHING LIMITED, 47 BRITISH GROVE, LONDON W4.
ALL RIGHTS RESERVED. INTERNATIONAL COPYRIGHT SECURED.

down deep in my heart, _____ I hear it

play, _____ I feel it start, then melt a-

-way. _____ I hear mu - sic when I touch your

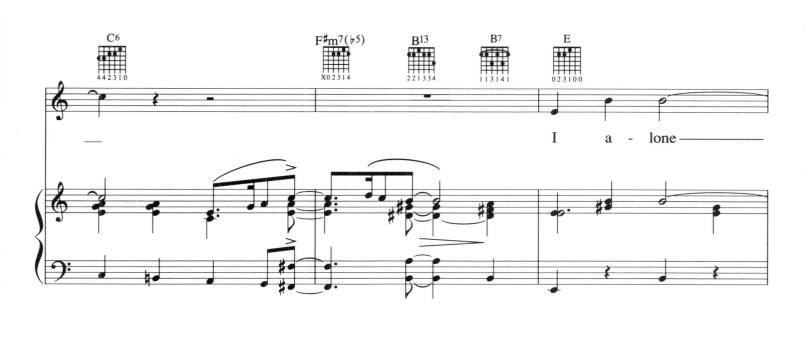

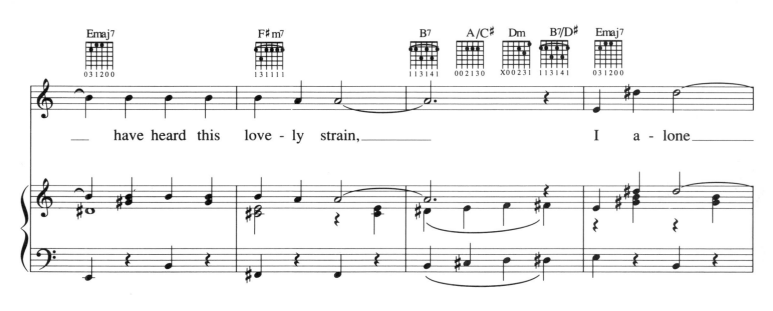

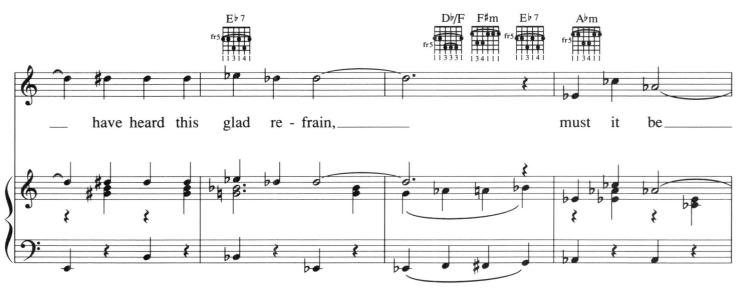

for - ev - er in - side of me, _____ why can't I

let it go, _____ why can't I let you know, _____ why can't I

let you know the song my heart would sing, _____ that beau - ti - ful

rhap - so - dy of love and youth and spring,_____ the mu - sic is

sweet,_____ the words are true,_____ the song is

you._____

The Music Goes Round And Around

Words by Red Hodgson. Music by Edward Farley & Michael Riley

© COPYRIGHT 1935 SELECT MUSIC PUBLICATIONS INCORPORATED, USA. RIGHTS
ASSIGNED TO JOY MUSIC INCORPORATED, USA.
CAMPBELL CONNELLY & COMPANY LIMITED, 8/9 FRITH STREET, LONDON W1.
ALL RIGHTS RESERVED. INTERNATIONAL COPYRIGHT SECURED.

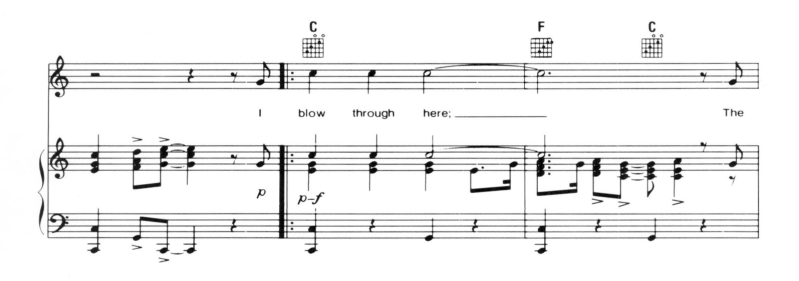

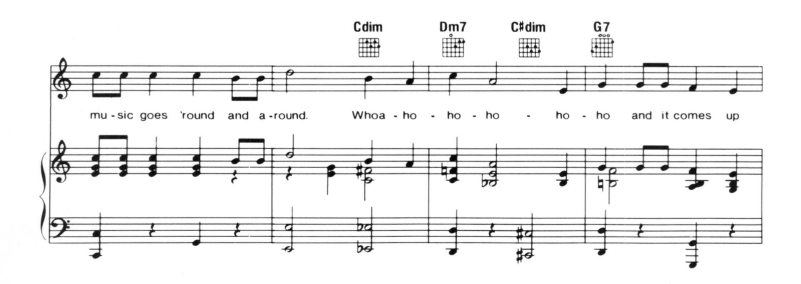

Tuxedo Junction

Words by Buddy Feyne
Music by Erskine Hawkins, William Johnson & Julian Dash

© COPYRIGHT LEWIS MUSIC PUBLISHING COMPANY INCORPORATED, USA.
AUTHORISED FOR SALE IN THE UNITED KINGDOM OF GREAT BRITAIN AND NORTHERN IRELAND
ONLY BY PERMISSION OF BOOSEY & HAWKES MUSIC PUBLISHERS LIMITED.
ALL RIGHTS RESERVED. INTERNATIONAL COPYRIGHT SECURED.

Yesterdays

Music by Jerome Kern. Words by Otto Harbach

© COPYRIGHT 1933 T.B. HARMS & COMPANY INCORPORATED, USA.
POLYGRAM MUSIC PUBLISHING LIMITED, 47 BRITISH GROVE, LONDON W4.
ALL RIGHTS RESERVED. INTERNATIONAL COPYRIGHT SECURED.